FACE TO FACE WITH

ELEPHANTS

by Beverly and Dereck Joubert

NATIONAL
GEOGRAPHIC
WASHINGTON, D.C.

We've lived and worked with elephants—and dodged getting flattened by them—for over 25 years. But I still relish each moment we spend in their company.

FACE TO FACE

She came out at us like a rocket! She was hot, angry, and very large—a full-grown elephant with a look in her eye that showed she meant business. I suspected there were going to be a few bruises, some tears, a little blood—all of them ours.

My wife, Beverly, and I were looking for elephants. Photographing wildlife can lead you into some scary places. We were in a wild area in Botswana, far from civilization. When we heard splashing noises at a nearby river, we walked down to it, hoping to find

Large, gray, and in a bad mood. When this elephant came at us out of nowhere, I knew we were going down!

THE SCOOP ON ELEPHANT POOP

Elephants are important to life in Africa, and so is their poop!

▬ Many trees have hard seeds. After elephants eat them and expel them, they are softened and ready to germinate.

▬ Flowery acacias and tall date palms grow along old elephant paths. Can you guess why?

▬ Baboons, birds, and insects raid the warm dung for seeds and other tasty treats. Yum!

▬ I use dung, too, to track elephants. I poke my finger into it. If it's still warm, that means the elephant is close by.

a herd of elephants. I spotted only three elephants, so we returned to our truck. We had removed the doors so we could get in and out silently. But this time, the springs groaned. Suddenly, the elephants at the river fell silent. They had heard us.

The forest brush exploded as the elephant cow charged at us wildly, head down, like a giant bulldozer. I started the engine, which will usually stop an elephant, but she didn't even hesitate. I was afraid she was going to ram the truck, so I slipped it out of gear. This way, it would roll easily when she hit it, and she wouldn't get hurt.

The truck shuddered as she rammed it. She was about an arm's length away—so close that I smelled her breath. Towering above us, she heaved with all her might, pushing us backward down the track.

Then I remembered that there were deep holes behind us. If she pushed us into one of them, we would tip over. I applied the brakes, and for the first time she couldn't move the truck. Now she was really mad. She lunged at the truck, smacking it hard and showering us with saliva. Chunks of ivory shot in at us like bullets when she chipped the tip of her tusk. This stopped her. She felt the chip with the tip of her

trunk, flapped her huge ears, and turned away.

We looked at each other and back at the elephant. Now we could see why she had attacked us. Under her chest was a cyst, a covered-over wound that can be painful. Elephants' thick skins heal fast, often trapping infections inside. Eventually, the infection can kill them. The wound looked as if it had been made by a bullet or spear. She had probably been attacked by poachers.

As we watched her go, I silently apologized on behalf of whoever had done that to her. We forgave her for coming face to face with us in such a rage.

Herds are often made up of individuals of different sizes. With binoculars, we scan them and check the various ages. You can see which years were good for breeding by counting the animals of each size.

7

MEET

The world is new for this little boy, who's just over a year old. Young ones like to explore, charging and chasing other creatures all over the savanna.

THE ELEPHANT

A very large male, like this one, can be terrifying, but some old males in their 60s are very calm. They spend their days munching on the soft river grasses in peace.

I don't like being charged by an elephant. It ruins the trust that we spend so much time trying to establish. We try to be invisible, going about our work in the hope that they will ignore us, giving us time to understand them.

Elephants are wild and difficult to tame. They've got attitude, and I like that. At the same time, they are the gentle giants of Africa.

They care for each other in amazing ways. We once saw a baby elephant trapped in mud.

The whole herd worked together to dig him out, lift him up, and carve a ramp so he could climb free.

In an area with many poachers, we have seen elephants whose trunks had been cut off by traps, or snares. They survive only because others in the herd tear down branches and feed them.

They are also very social. It's fascinating to sit near them, just listening. There is a constant rumble, soft and very comforting. Everyone used to think these sounds were just indigestion. But thanks to scientist Katy Payne, we now know the elephants

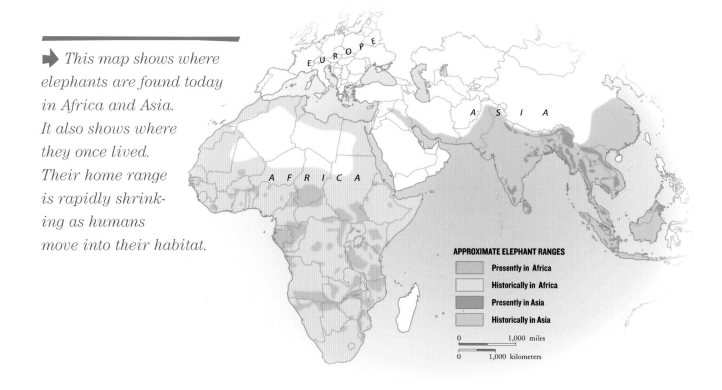

➡ *This map shows where elephants are found today in Africa and Asia. It also shows where they once lived. Their home range is rapidly shrinking as humans move into their habitat.*

APPROXIMATE ELEPHANT RANGES

Presently in Africa
Historically in Africa
Presently in Asia
Historically in Asia

0   1,000 miles
0   1,000 kilometers

are communicating. In addition to the sounds we can hear, they make low-frequency sounds that we can't hear. Payne used giant speakers and recorded hundreds of hours of elephant calls. When she replayed them for us, elephants drinking peacefully nearby swung around and fanned their ears to listen!

You cannot look into an elephant's eyes and not feel that there is a deep intelligence there, something ancient and thoughtful.

This massive bull elephant, a symbol of Africa, stands like a giant on the plains. Elephants once roamed the continent from sea to sea.

11

LIFE

For years we had hoped to be there at a moment like this. And one hot October day, we finally witnessed the birth of a baby elephant!

AS AN ELEPHANT

An elephant herd is made up of members of an extended family. This closely bonded group consists of the adult females and their offspring. The average herd in Botswana has 8–15 individuals.

The elephant's birth: It starts with a long drop to earth into a crumpled-up heap. The newborn looks like a miniature elephant in oversize skin, with feet that don't quite match or fit. Elephant babies may be funny looking, but the whole herd celebrates the birth. There is a lot of trumpeting and wailing. Everyone comes to see the little bundle of wrinkles, usually sniffing it with their trunks, probably to see if it is a boy or a girl.

The little one puts up with all this prodding and

The baby was wobbly for about 20 minutes and then followed his mother off into life as an elephant. His weight at birth is about 220 pounds (100 kg)—just less than what his mother consumes in food each day!

jostling, but all it really wants to do is figure out where the milk is. That milk is in an udder between the front legs of its mom.

Pretty soon the baby is running (stumbling, really) alongside its mother. The herd takes giant steps. For each step an adult takes, the baby has to take 10 or 12 steps just to keep up. It looks exhausting!

Shortly after, the real fun starts. Baby elephants soon realize they can bully everyone else on the savanna and in the forests. They chase everything from small cattle egrets to big buffalo, and all creatures in between. Young elephants stay near their mothers for several years.

Between 12 and 15 years of age, the young females start attracting males and are able to mate. Around this time, they take on the role of *allomother,* or babysitter, helping to look after an older female's babies. Perhaps this is training for when they have babies of their own.

For mating to succeed, both male and female have to be ready. The male's period of readiness is called *musth.* If mating is successful, the female will give birth to a single calf 22 months later.

◀ *The leader, or matriarch, guards her family by gathering them behind her at any sign of danger. She fans out her ears to make herself look even larger than she is and scares off the attacker.*

Height at shoulder

Adult Male
11–12 feet
(3.3 m - 3.6 m)

Adult Female
8–9 feet
(2.4 m -
2.7 m)

Baby
3 feet
(1 m)

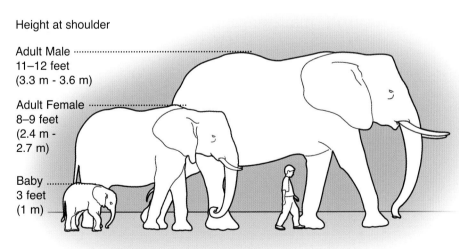

◀ *Compare the sizes of elephants to a three-and-a-half-foot-tall child. A mature elephant bull is up to 12 feet (3.6 m) tall at the shoulder. Females are much smaller, up to 9 feet (2.7 m) tall. A baby that can walk under its mother's belly without ducking is less than a year old.*

Young males begin to drift a little farther from the herd as they get older. Usually this lagging behind ends with grumpy rumbles when they realize that no one stops and waits for them. But eventually the young bulls do leave the herd. With elephants, this is a gradual, gentle process. No one forces them away.

The young males join groups of mature bull elephants, old guys who lumber through the

Calves born around the same time, like these cousins, often grow quite close.

ELEPHANTS HAVE A LOT TO SAY

Elephants have vocal cords in their throats and a special pouch beneath their tongues. They use these to communicate.

▬ By studying elephant behavior together with recordings of their calls, scientists have figured out the meaning of about 50 calls.

▬ Some elephant talk is at too low a frequency for us to hear, but elephants also make loud trumpet calls you can hear a mile away!

▬ You may not be able to hear them, but if you are quiet, you may be able to *feel* them talking. It's as if something is vibrating in your chest.

forest from waterhole to waterhole, smashing down trees to feed on and fearing nothing (except humans). This connection between young bulls and older bulls is vital. If young bulls grow up without the supervision of the older bulls, they get aggressive and nasty. In several instances, gangs of young "orphan" males in wildlife parks attacked and killed buffalo and rhino. It gave conservation managers a headache trying to figure out a way to control them. Finally, the managers introduced a few old bull elephants. Within a short time, the bulls took control, slapped the young males into shape, and formed a well-behaved herd.

The heads of extended elephant families are called matriarchs. Matriarchs are mature females who lead rich family groups. The great selflessness of these matriarchs is clear when there is the slightest hint of danger. We've seen

▼ *If there is a true King of the Beasts, it must be the bull elephant. Everyone runs from him!*

elephants respond to threats all too often. The matriarch leader signals to her herd to gather around and behind her. She lifts her head up three feet (one meter) or more. Then the matriarch steps out, head held high, ears out wide, ready to take on the attackers. She dips forward and charges, with the entire herd behind her.

It's a strategy that scares off most things. Sadly, it is a terrible defense when humans are the threat.

(left) Elephants seem to set aside time for play. On a sweltering day in Botswana (120°F; 49°C), swimming is the perfect way to chill out!

(right) Lions often stake out waterholes and the areas nearby, where herds are most desperate for water. They launch their attacks on stragglers and lone calves.

At Elephant Back Safaris, Beverly developed a particularly close bond with a small, trained elephant called Seba. He was the star of a film we made called Whispers: An Elephant's Tale.

ROOM TO ROAM

Along the Chobe River, elephants are so calm that they move around you quite comfortably, making you feel like part of the family. It's times like this that we live for—a shared moment between two species.

About 50 or 60 years ago, nearly two million elephants existed. Today, there are fewer than 500,000 left. Poachers seeking their long, gleaming ivory tusks are responsible for many of the deaths. Governments and even conservation groups have also killed elephants over the past few decades to control their numbers. When too many elephants live in a small area, the land is over-grazed and put under a lot of stress.

Some say the practice of controlling their numbers,

It is now rare to find places in Africa that have enough space for large herds of elephants. In Botswana, however, they can roam over huge tracts of land in and around the Okavango Delta.

called culling, is still needed. To do this, rangers challenge the herd and wait for the lead female to gather the members. Then they kill her. Without her, the herd is easy to destroy.

Most conservationists today have better ways to manage elephants. In Botswana there are about 100,000 elephants or more. (It's hard to get an

An elephant investigates the bones of a fallen friend. Sometimes elephants toss earth or branches over dead elephant bodies. It can't be scientifically proven, but we think they feel sad when they lose a friend or loved one.

accurate count because they move around.) But officials here don't cull the herds, nor should they. Many conservationists believe that the reserves and parks should be redesigned so that the elephants can travel along corridors, or safe roads, from one reserve to another. For example, in Angola, reserves have few elephants, so linking the reserves will ease the pressure on overcrowded areas elsewhere.

Some research suggests that elephants are clever enough to understand when there are too many of them and start adjusting their own breeding rates. I am not sure whether this is true, but ongoing research should tell us.

Lions are another threat to elephants. It is sad to see a lion kill an elephant, but it is nature's way. In Botswana, where we live, it seems to be happening more often. This is probably because the elephant population there is high, and when it comes to hunting, lions take advantage of any opportunity. Still, lions take just a fraction of the elephants.

Elephants sometimes cause problems for farmers, who don't like having their crops raided. In a single night, one elephant can wipe out enough corn to feed a human family for a whole year. Instead of

An elephant known locally as Abu. He is a wonderful character and a giant in the world of giants.

reacting violently, some people started growing chili plants, which are hot and spicy, around their other crops. Sure enough, elephants stayed away.

Photographic safaris (ecotourism) can help bring money to local people. This helps them see a real benefit from elephants. When the elephants are "paying" for schools and clinics, people will be more inclined to protect them and respect their corridors.

So the future for elephants could be very good, but they need space. By respecting these gentle giants and protecting the great open spaces they need, we help the Earth and enrich our own lives, too.

We once showed a film we did on elephants to the president of Botswana. Afterward, he held Beverly's hand and said, "Why can't we be more like elephants?" The words often ring in my mind. Yes, I wish we could be more like elephants too. It will help us share the future together.

HOW YOU CAN HELP

━━ Don't buy or use ivory. Ivory belongs to elephants. Most people are shocked to discover that someone has to kill an elephant to create an ivory bracelet. You can gently let people know that an elephant had to die to provide that piece of ivory or trinket.

━━ Write to your representatives in Congress, asking them to strengthen the bans on trading in ivory. Let's not buy and sell products from dead wildlife!

━━ Refuse to go to circuses and shows that use trained elephants. Even if the trainers aren't cruel, these animals are usually not allowed to live as they should, in groups, or with lots of room to move around outdoors.

━━ Spend some time in the company of elephants, even in a zoo, and just "be" with them. You may find that spending time with these gentle giants makes you feel better. It works for me! I realize that we are not alone as intelligent beings on this planet. I feel more whole, more connected to the world.

━━ The World Wildlife Fund and the African Wildlife Foundation are just two of the groups that support elephant research and make life better for wild elephants. Find out about their work at www.worldwildlife.org and www.afw.org. Maybe your family would like to contribute to these groups.

━━ Read all you can about elephants. Tell your friends and family about all you've learned. Knowledge starts with a small seed being planted.

← *Twins are rare. They occur less than once in a hundred elephant births, and seeing them is a real treat. One elephant baby is a lot of work for its mother, so I doubt twins are much of a treat for her! She will have to eat constantly for years to provide enough milk for them.*

IT'S YOUR TURN

Would you like to see and photograph elephants yourself? You can start by visiting a wildlife park, or a zoo. Try to find one where the elephants are not separated into pens but are allowed to live as a group and spend most of their time outdoors.

⬇ *The trunk, weird as it is, evolved as a combination of the nose and the top lip.*

1 Make a list of the kinds of things you would like to show. It could be the ways they use their trunks to eat and explore their world. Or how mothers and babies interact—a large zoo may have a mother and baby in residence. Or how elephants enjoy playing in a pool or even splashing water around in a tub.

2 Get out your camera and notebook! Remember that elephants are sensitive creatures. Never try to get their attention by waving or throwing things, making loud noises, or acting wild. Never take a flash picture right in an animal's face. Stand quietly and observe. You will learn a lot

without even trying. Use your notebook to write about what you see. Sometimes signs tell you the names, ages, and background of the elephants.

3 National Geographic has a video game called "Afrika" that we helped with. It's a cool way to go on a virtual safari!

4 In Africa, there are many opportunities to see elephants living wild and free. If you are lucky enough to visit, Botswana and Kenya are the best places to see elephants. In Selinda Reserve, Botswana, there are around 9,000 elephants. They stream down to the river at midday. What a sight! In Kenya, Amboseli National Reserve is great. We saw massive elephants at a lodge near there.

FACTS AT A GLANCE

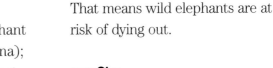

Scientific Name
Loxodonta africana

Common Names Elephant (English); Tlou (Setswana); Nglovo (Zulu); and in East Africa, Tembo (Swahili).

Population
Elephants move around and are hard to count. The International Union for Conservation and Natural Resources estimates there are less than 500,000 of

them left in Africa. It classifies African elephants as "vulnerable." That means wild elephants are at risk of dying out.

Size
African elephants are the largest species of land animal. Adult males are up to 12 feet (3.6 m) tall at the shoulder. Females are up to 9 feet (2.7 m) tall. Adult males weigh up to 16,535 lbs (7,500 kg), females up to 7,125 lbs (3,232 kg).

Lifespan
In the wild, elephants live 60 to 70 years. In zoos, elephants can live up to 80 years.

Special Features
The elephant's trunk, with more than 50,000 muscles along its length, is an amazingly useful part of its body. First, of course, it is a nose, used for breathing and for smelling things. The sensitive tip can also curl like fingers to pick up objects as small as toothpicks. But the trunk is also strong enough to uproot a tree. Elephants use their trunks to

← *The Asian elephant,* Elephas maximus *(top), has small ears, a large head, and thin tusks. It is only distantly related to the African elephant,* Loxodonta africana *(bottom). African elephants have large ears— shaped like Africa!—and carry their heads level with their shoulders.*

stroke each other, smack opponents, and throw objects around. They even use them as snorkels, holding the tips in the air while they swim underwater.

Adult elephants of both sexes grow tusks, which developed from specialized teeth. They use their tusks to defend themselves, but also to dig up plants, salt, and minerals that they eat, or to dig holes in the sand for water. Elephants favor a right or left tusk, just as you favor your right or left hand.

Elephants' feet look big, but they actually walk on the tips of their toes. Most of the foot acts as a soft cushion. A whole herd of elephants can travel very quietly when they want to.

Elephants' skin is tough and thick, but they don't have much hair to shield them from the sun. That's one reason they roll in mud. It acts as a sunscreen and protects their skin.

Habitat

In East and southern Africa, elephants live on the grasslands, or savannas. Forest elephants live in West and central Africa. In Namibia, elephants live in the desert. These tall elephants survive on very little water. In the wetlands area in Botswana, they virtually live in water, bathing every day. Elephants are protected in many parks and reserves throughout Africa.

Food

Grass, fruit, palm nuts, tree bark and stems, leaves—lots of them. In fact, elephants eat around 400 pounds (200 kg) of plant material a day. They drink up to 60 gallons (225 liters) of water. They eat no meat at all.

Reproduction

Mating takes place over a week when both male and female are ready. Female pregnancy, or gestation, lasts a long time— 22 months. She nurtures and suckles the calf for two more years before mating again. This means that elephants can breed every four years at most. Young elephants stay near their mothers for several years. Females remain with the same family group all their lives.

Social Habits

Wild elephants live in groups of related individuals, led by a mature female. Young males leave the herd, joining other bulls or living alone. Elephants usually follow regular routes from one grazing area to another, or move with the seasons to find the best feeding grounds. They travel and feed both night and day. Elephants communicate across distances with low-frequency rumbling calls. They seem to have very good memories for places, other elephants, and people. They also keep track of where other elephants are by scenting them on the wind, or checking out piles of dung.

Biggest Threats

Except for lions, elephants are not hunted by most predators. Growing human presence on wild lands in Africa threatens elephants when people want land for crops. Poachers who hunt elephants for ivory have caused the greatest drop in the elephant population.

GLOSSARY

Allomother: a female elephant who cares for another elephant's offspring.

Bull: a male elephant.

Calf: a baby elephant up to around 12 years old.

Charge: the forward rush of an attacking elephant.

Cow: a female elephant.

Ivory: the material that animals' teeth are made of. Elephant tusks are especially sought after.

Low-frequency sound: sound below the range that most humans can detect. Many animals can hear low-frequency or very high-frequency sounds that we can't hear.

Matriarch: the female head of a family or extended family.

Musth: a state of readiness for mating in male elephants. Musth bulls can be a little cranky and tend to charge more often than males not in this phase.

Poaching: the illegal killing of a protected animal.

Tusks: incisor teeth that grow curving out of the upper lips of elephants. Tusks can be ten feet long.

FIND OUT MORE

Books & Articles
Douglas-Hamilton, Iain and Oria. *Among the Elephants.* New York, NY: Penguin, 1978.

Joubert, Dereck and Beverly. *African Diaries.* Washington, D.C.: National Geographic, 2000.

Joubert, Dereck and Beverly. *Whispers: The Story of a Baby Elephant.* New York, NY: Hyperion Press, 1999.

Moss, Cynthia, and Colbeck, Martyn. *Echo of the Elephants.* New York, NY: William Morrow, 1993.

Poole, Joyce. *Coming of Age with Elephants.* New York, NY: Hyperion Press, 1996.

Films
Whispers: An Elephant's Tale. Walt Disney, 2000.

Reflections on Elephants, by Dereck and Beverly Joubert, National Geographic Television, 2000.

Web Sites
www.wildlifeconservationfilms.com

www.awf.org/content/wildlife/detail/elephant

www.iucn.org

www.sandiegozoo.org/animalbytes/t-elephant.html

RESEARCH & PHOTOGRAPHIC NOTES

I've already told you how to start understanding elephants, and I think this is what it takes, really, getting to know your subject. We've known great photographers and filmmakers, but it's the people who have empathy for elephants that achieve the best images. What we like to do is get down low, much lower than the elephant's line of vision. We do this to accentuate the tremendous size of these animals. I love to see them up against the sky, rather than cluttered against the brush.

Beverly uses Canon cameras and a vehicle full of lenses. You wouldn't think you could use anything other than a wide angle lens really, given the size of these creatures!

I will always remember something I used to do as a kid with my brother, who is an artist. We took a picture of an elephant and cut it in half. He took a piece and so did I. We both had fairly good representations of the elephant. We cut our halves in half again. We could still see elephants. We cut again and again until we finally looked up at each other, realizing that we'd gone too far. But we had also done what Japanese artists are so good at, finding the most iconic picture, the very essence of that animal or image.

With this in mind, both Beverly and I compose our pictures as minimalistically as possible. This is a great discipline, to find the one part of an animal that represents the whole species. Play with framing just the one thing that *is* an elephant—no, not the dung!—but the tusk and maybe that wise old eye. Light that and compose for just that. It's haunting and tells a story at the same time. It is mysterious, but not so weird that you have to look at it for days to figure out what it is.

Africa, life—everything, really—is made up of small details. Many of them just symbolize the whole.   —DJ

FOR THE GIANTS THAT COME
BEFORE US: THE ELEPHANTS,
CYNTHIA MOSS, JOYCE POOLE,
IAIN DOUGLAS-HAMILTON, KATY
PAYNE, RICHARD LEAKEY . . . ALL
AMBASSADORS AND WONDERFUL
FRIENDS OF ELEPHANTS. —DJ & BJ

Acknowledgments
Our first thank-you goes to an elephant
cow that charged and hit us hard one
night, upended us, and left us shaken but
alive. She changed our lives and made us
live one day at a time. We have been
inspired by some great elephant people:
Iain Douglas-Hamilton, whose book I was
reading when I first decided to work in
the bush; Joyce Poole; Cynthia Moss;
Katy Payne; the owners of Wilderness
Safaris, in whose reserve we live and
work; the President and people of
Botswana; the Ministry of Environment
and its Department of Wildlife and
National Parks for permitting us to do
our work. The National Geographic
Society has inspired us and so many others worldwide with its work. For years
the Society has supported our research,
photography, and filming, but only
recently have we become fully aware of
the extent of its efforts to inspire people
to care for the planet. Last, to the
elephants: Dear Sir/Madam, we are sorry
for what we humans have done to you.
—Dereck and Beverly Joubert

Back cover photograph by Jacques
Nortier (copyright Wildlife Films).

Book design by David M. Seager.
The body text of the book is set in
ITC Century. The display text is set
in Knockout and Party Noid.

*Published by the
National Geographic Society*

John M. Fahey, Jr., *President and
   Chief Executive Officer*

Gilbert M. Grosvenor,
   Chairman of the Board

Tim T. Kelly,
   President, Global Media Group

Nina D. Hoffman, *Executive Vice
   President; President, Book
   Publishing Group*

Staff for This Book

Nancy Laties Feresten, *Vice President,
   Editor-in-Chief of Children's Books*

Bea Jackson, *Design and Illustrations
   Director, Children's Books*

Amy Shields, *Executive Editor*

Jennifer Emmett, Mary Beth Oelkers-
Keegan, *Project Editors*

David M. Seager, *Art Director*

Lori Epstein, *Illustrations Editor*

Jocelyn G. Lindsay, *Researcher*

Dianne Hosmer, *Indexer*

Carl Mehler, *Director of Maps*

Rebecca Baines, *Editorial Assistant*

Jennifer Thornton, *Managing Editor*

Grace Hill, *Associate Managing Editor*

R. Gary Colbert, *Production Director*

Lewis R. Bassford, *Production Manager*

Maryclare Tracy, Nicole Elliott,
   Manufacturing Managers

Susan Borke, *Legal and Business Affairs*

Front cover & pages 2–3: Face to face
with an African elephant; *front flap:* An elephant calf; *back cover:* Dereck and Beverly
Joubert with one of Africa's gentle giants;
page one: A young elephant raises its trunk,
sniffing out danger.

Library of Congress
Cataloging-in-Publication Data

Joubert, Beverly.
 Face to face with elephants / by Beverly and
Dereck Joubert.
    p. cm.
ISBN 978-1-4263-0325-8 (trade)—
ISBN 978-1-4263-0326-5 (library)
1. African elephant. 2. African elephant—
Pictorial works. I. Joubert, Dereck. II.
Title. QL737.P98J67 2008
599.67—dc22

2007041229

Founded in 1888, the National Geographic
Society is one of the largest nonprofit scientific and educational organizations in the
world. It reaches more than 285 million
people worldwide each month through its
official journal, NATIONAL GEOGRAPHIC, and
its four other magazines; the National
Geographic Channel; television documen-
taries; radio programs; films; books; videos
and DVDs; maps; and interactive media.
National Geographic has funded more than
8,000 scientific research projects and
supports an education program combating
geographic illiteracy.

For more information, please call
1-800-NGS LINE (647-5463)
or write to the following address:

National Geographic Society
1145 17th Street N.W.
Washington, D.C. 20036-4688 U.S.A.

Visit us online at
www.nationalgeographic.com/books.
Librarians and teachers, visit us at
www.ngchildrensbooks.com. Kids and parents,
visit us at kids.nationalgeographic.com.

For information about special discounts
for bulk purchases, please contact
National Geographic Books Special Sales:
ngspecsales@ngs.org. For rights or permis-
sions inquiries, please contact National
Geographic Books Subsidiary Rights:
ngbookrights@ngs.org.

Printed in China

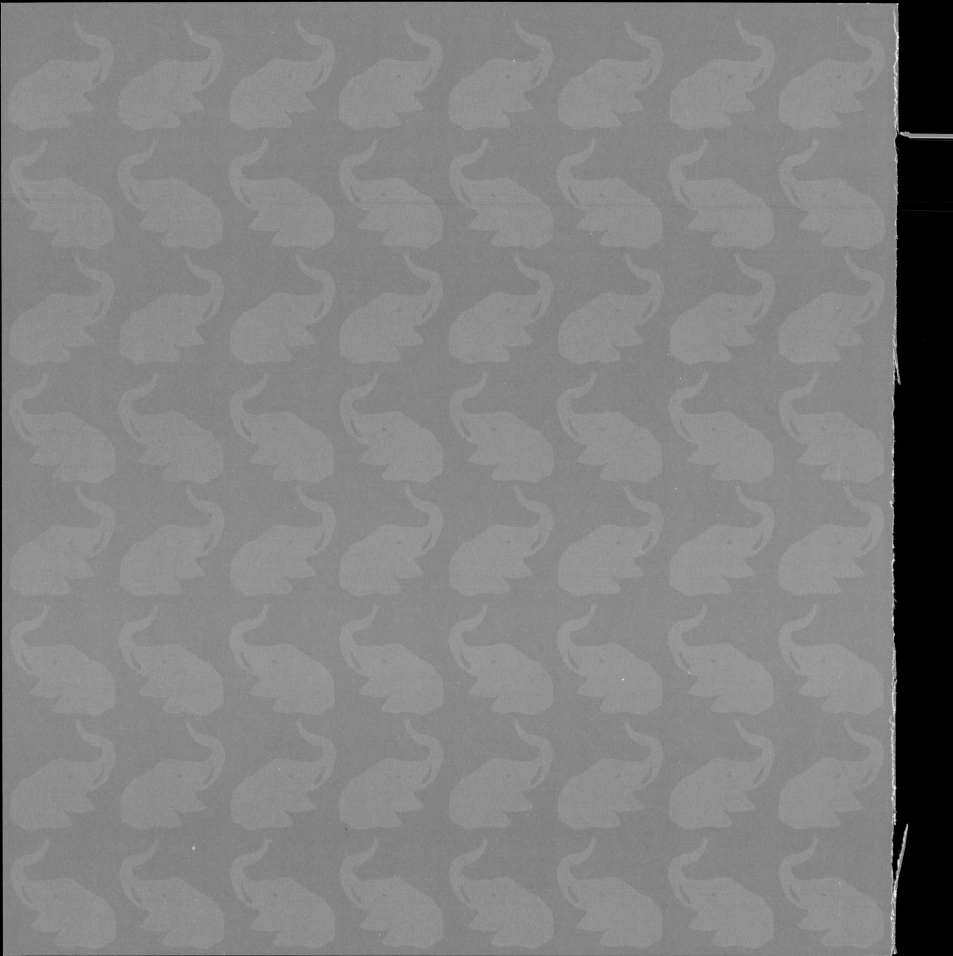

LIFE UNDER ICE

MARY M. CERULLO

PHOTOGRAPHY BY
BILL CURTSINGER

TILBURY HOUSE, PUBLISHERS
GARDINER, MAINE

ANTARCTICA

A N T A R C T I C A

Since Antarctica was discovered in 1820, scientists and researchers have braved gale-force winds, mountainous waves, thick fog, and giant icebergs to study one of the few wild places left in our world. Antarctica is a land of extremes—the coldest, driest, windiest, and highest continent. Its name—Antarctica—means the opposite of the Arctic. Ninety percent of the world's ice and 70 percent of the world's fresh water is frozen in antarctic glaciers up to two miles thick. (If they were broken up, there would be enough to supply every person on earth with an ice cube as large as the Great Pyramid!) In the winter, this continent at the bottom of the earth doubles in size as sea ice spreads out from the coast for thousands of miles.

On the surface, Antarctica is a frozen desert. But beneath the sea ice lies a strange oasis, home to an amazing variety of animals and plants that thrive in sub-freezing water, sheltered by the ice that covers their home like a glass roof.

Nature photographer Bill Curtsinger has traveled to this frozen continent many times to dive in its chilly waters and learn about creatures that are able to live in water that is as cold as it can get before you have to walk on it. His dives beneath the ice are adventures in science and survival.

On this trip, Bill and a research team board a helicopter at McMurdo Station, the main center for scientists in Antarctica. The helicopter will drop them off 50 miles away near the edge of the frozen McMurdo Sound. Bill, Paul Dayton from the Scripps Institution of Oceanography, and two other dive partners are planning to study and photograph the animals that live on the bottom of the Southern Ocean—the benthic life.

An emperor penguin watches new arrivals.

When you dive in Antarctica, you don't just tumble off the side of a boat—or you might end up with a concussion. First you must drill through 5 to 10 feet of sea ice. In the past, underwater explorers used chain saws and dynamite to create diving holes. Today divers use machine-powered augers to drill neat, round tunnels.

Bill and his team land near a breathing hole left by a Weddell seal. The seal had found a crack in the ice, and with its sharp, protruding teeth it chiseled a hole to reach the surface to breathe. This makes the divers' first task easier—all they have to do is enlarge on the Weddell seal's work.

The fur seal (left) and the Weddell seal (right) are two of Antarctica's marine mammals.

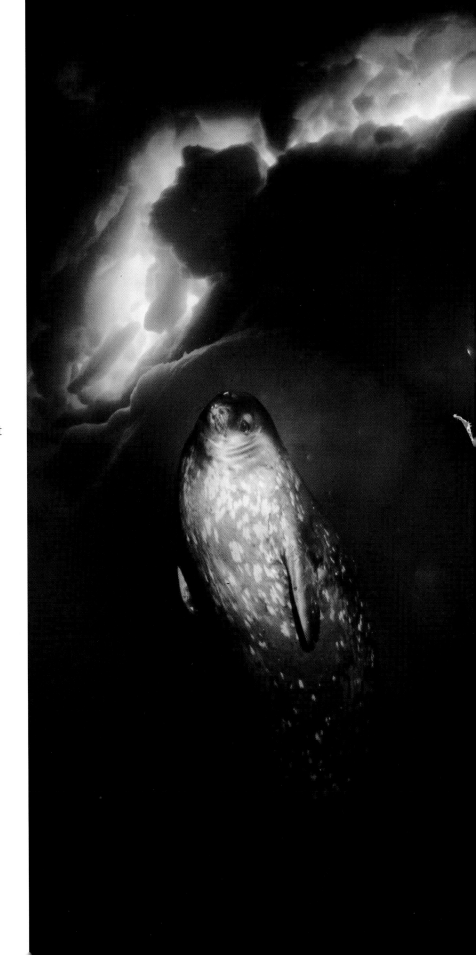

To prepare for his dive, Bill wriggles into his dry suit, a well-insulated dive suit that doesn't allow water to get next to his skin like a regular wet suit does. The dry suit covers all of his body except his face and hands. He pulls on insulated gloves that look like giant mittens. Then he slips on his flippers and mask and lifts his dive tank. He gives his dive companions a thumbs-up to show that he is ready to go.

As Bill drops down through the crack in the ice he feels a little like Alice in Wonderland falling down the rabbit's hole. He can't help gasping at the cold water. His lips and cheeks—the only exposed parts of his body—go numb, and within a few seconds his head starts to ache from the cold. Even in summer, water temperatures average 29°F (-1.5°C) to 35.4°F (1.9°C).

WHY DOESN'T THE OCEAN FREEZE?

The water temperature around Antarctica ranges from 28°F (-1.9°C) to 35.4°F (1.9°C). Fresh water freezes at 32°F (0°C). Salt water freezes at a lower temperature because the dissolved salt blocks the water molecules from linking to form ice crystals. Sea water eventually freezes around 28°F (-1.9°C). (It also melts at a lower temperature, which is why road crews salt icy roads in winter.)

In the ocean, the salt is left in the water during the freezing process. This makes antarctic water saltier than most of the world's oceans.

WINTER OR SUMMER?

When it's winter in the Northern Hemisphere, it is summer in Antarctica. Summer temperatures around the coast average a balmy 32°F (0°C). Winter air temperatures hover around -60°F (-51°C). It's so cold that ice cream stored outside has to be microwaved before it can be eaten!

They are making this dive in October—which is early spring in Antarctica. The water is still as clear as a tropical sea, but by New Year's, when the sun is overhead twenty-four hours a day, billions of tiny floating plants called phytoplankton will be in full bloom. They form a thick sea soup, and Bill would barely be able to see his hand in front of his face. But now, after six months of darkness (May through August), there isn't enough plankton to block Bill's view, and he can clearly see the diving hole from several hundred feet away.

The sun illuminates the open water of the hole like a spotlight. Bill and his dive partners turn back frequently to make sure the hole is still in sight—it's their only link to the world above. Should Bill lose track of the hole, he will retrace his route until his escape hatch is once more in view. Bill shivers—not just from the cold, but as he imagines being trapped beneath a solid ceiling of ice.

Almost immediately a Weddell seal spies Bill. Like an eager puppy, it dashes over to size him up. The curious seal moves in for a closer look until it is nose to nose with Bill's face mask. It circles the divers for a few minutes before swooping past them to poke its head through the dive hole for a quick breath. Then it plunges into deeper water.

The divers also descend, but much more slowly than the seal. Within seconds, the seal returns from the depths to check them out again.

Weddell seals can dive deep and then surface quickly because they don't get the bends like humans do. The bends—also called decompression sickness—are caused by nitrogen gas that becomes trapped in the blood. If a human diver returns to the surface too quickly, the change in pressure may release gas bubbles into the bloodstream that may burst and cause dizziness, paralysis, collapse, and even death. But as a Weddell seal dives, its rib cage partially collapses, squeezing air out of its lungs

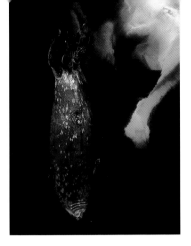

until it equalizes the pressure of the water above, keeping the dangerous gas bubbles from forming in its blood. Like whales, these seals store oxygen efficiently, and their blood is pumped away from their flippers to their heart, lungs, and brain where it is needed most.

Scientists have outfitted Weddell seals with instruments that record how deep they dive. They usually dive to 650-1,300 feet (200-400 meters), but can descend to almost 2,000 feet (600 meters) in search of fish, squid, and bottom animals. They can hold their breath for over an hour!

Bill stops a few feet above the ocean floor. It's a beautiful and haunting place, carpeted with sea anemones, sponges, sea stars, brittle stars, sea urchins, sea spiders, worms, and soft corals. It's as colorful as diving on a coral reef in the tropics, and Bill almost forgets how cold he is. As they swim along, Bill and his diving team are careful not to cause damage with their long flippers.

Out of the corner of his eye, Bill sees a chunk of ocean floor drifting slowly upward toward the surface. Unfolding before him is the answer to a mystery that used to puzzle scientists. Every so often someone would find a starfish or a sponge sitting on the surface of the sea ice. Since these bottom-dwellers can't swim, how did they get up there?

Scientists love to find the answer to a mystery! By careful observation they discovered that every spring, fresh water from melting ice pours off the land and the surface ice and sinks to the bottom of the ocean. Slightly colder than the surrounding salty water, this "anchor ice" freezes as soon as it touches a rock, mud, or an unlucky animal lying on the ocean bottom.

As the bits of anchor ice gradually merge, it becomes more buoyant and floats up, carrying sea stars, sponges, and an occasional slow-moving fish up through the water until they bump into the surface ice and freeze onto the underside of the ice. Gradually the ice above melts away, exposing the sea stars and other creatures that would normally be living on the ocean floor.

Far left: A diver watches as anchor ice floats toward the surface. Top: Colorful sea anemones cover the ocean floor.

11

Bill's diving team follows a slope down to a depth of about 120 feet (37 meters)—it's like taking a slow elevator down a twelve-story building. Paul is a benthic ecologist who is diving today to learn more about sponge growth in antarctic waters. He finds a giant sponge larger than himself, and while he measures it, Bill swims around him capturing shots of his work. Paul is careful not to push too hard on the sponge for fear of damaging its delicate structure.

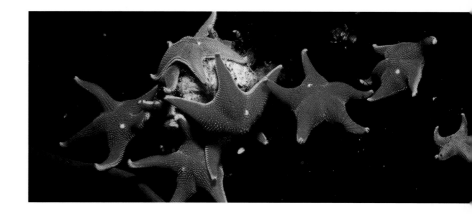

After about a half hour, Bill's hands and feet have grown numb. His fingers are so stiff he can no longer adjust the focus on his camera, so he signals his partners that it's time to go up. They rise up to a depth of 30 feet (9 meters), where they stop and allow their bodies to decompress for several minutes. Returning to their dive hole in the ice takes longer than they expect because distances in crystal-clear water seem much closer than they really are.

Diving in cold water uses much more energy than diving in warmer seas, and the divers rise to the surface completely exhausted. Bill and the others crawl into a tent and crank up a kerosene stove to get warm. They are going to spend three nights in the tent so they can make several more dives before returning to the science station. Each member of the team devours a stack of steaks, then settles into his or her thick, down sleeping bag.

Before turning off his headlamp, Bill writes down his thoughts and makes some quick sketches of the strange animals he has seen. He has a lot of questions to ask the scientists back at the science station and is looking forward to hearing their explanations and ideas.

Bill falls asleep soon, but he tosses and turns all night, and never really warms up. His dreams are jumbled with images of ice and snow. He wakes up before 6 A.M. The sun is still as bright as it was when they went to bed, but it's freezing cold in the tent. The condensation from their breath has formed a coating of rime ice inside the tent. Their toothpaste is frozen solid. The bravest one climbs out of his sleeping bag to start the stove. Soon the temperature inside the tent is bearable and coffee is made. Getting ready for another dive, Bill reminds himself that the water under the ice will be warmer than the air above.

Bill and the dive team spend four days out on the sea ice before the helicopter comes to take them back to McMurdo Station. After a long, hot shower and a huge meal at headquarters, Bill pulls out his journal and peppers the scientists sitting around the table with his questions. A geologist, a marine biologist, a meteorologist, a physical oceanographer, an astronomer, and even a veterinarian are all working on various projects at the science station.

Bill has dived in all the seas of the world, but diving in Antarctica still amazes him. Nowhere else do marine animals face the challenges they have to contend with under the ice. Here, they have to swim in water cold enough to freeze their blood. It is dark for six months of the year, and without sunlight to fuel plankton growth, plant-eaters have no food. Bottom animals risk becoming trapped in anchor ice. Air-breathing seals have to find holes just to breath. Penguins sometimes commute hundreds of miles between their nesting sites and the sea to find food for their chicks.

Krill are shrimp-like animals eaten by most of the
other animals in Antarctica's marine foodweb.

Bill asks the scientists around the table, "Why do
the animals put up with the cold and ice?" The
researchers, digging into a plate of freshly baked
cookies, respond in a chorus, "FOOD!"

The Southern Ocean is like a giant food factory,
they explain to Bill between bites. Strong currents
act like a spoon in a pot, stirring up a thick soup of
nutrients. Minerals from melting glaciers mix with
decaying plants and animals from the ocean floor,
and when you add abundant sunlight, you have

ideal conditions for an underwater greenhouse.
Tiny plants called ice algae grow in pockets on
the underside of sea ice, and phytoplankton—
microscopic floating plants—bloom in the water
near the surface. These are eaten by shrimp-like
creatures called krill. Each krill is only the size of
a human thumb, but when there are thousands
of them together, they can turn the ocean pink.

There isn't much variety to eat in Antarctica—
the food web is simple—so krill are very important.
Penguins, squid, fish, seals, seabirds, and even
enormous whales all eat a steady diet of krill.

Bill has spotted several kinds of whales swimming
in the open water surrounding the antarctic
continent. Well insulated from the cold by thick
layers of blubber, killer whales, minkes, humpbacks,
finbacks, and even the giant blue whales feast on
the krill. In fact, the word "krill" is the Norwegian
term for "whale food."

Bill doodles a picture of a krill on his napkin, which prompts him to recall the sketch he made in his notebook of an animal on the ocean floor that he couldn't identify. He turns to Paul Dayton sitting at the far end of the table and asks, "What was that huge, prehistoric-looking 'bug'? It seemed familiar, but I've never seen one so big—it looked like something you'd see in an Age of Dinosaurs diorama in a natural history museum."

Paul laughs and replies that what Bill saw was a giant isopod, an animal related to a shrimp. Bill is amazed. He's seen thousands of isopods wriggling around in rocky tidepools, but each was only the size of a fingernail. "This isopod had to be five inches long!"

Top left: Giants of the Antarctica include a giant isopod and (bottom) a giant sea spider.

Paul explains that it's a phenomenon called "gigantism" found in extremely cold seas. Here in Antarctica you can find sea spiders as large as dinner plates, jellyfish the size of umbrellas, sponges big enough to stand inside, and sea stars almost two feet across!

"Maybe it's because the animals have found a habitat that no one else wanted, so there's no competition for food or space," suggests another scientist. "With less pressure from competitors and predators, they don't have to rush growing up so they grow large, if slowly." Paul explains that the cold water slows their body functions and leads to a longer lifespan. One starfish was known to have lived thirty-nine years!

"Cold-blooded animals also move slower in frigid water," points out Allan Child, a scientist from the Smithsonian Institution who is studying sea spiders. Even ice fish and giant isopods move so slowly they have been caught in anchor ice. Bill remembers watching sea spiders (called pycnogonids) creep slowly across the ocean floor on their spindly legs. "They're the original slow-motion animals," agrees Allan. "You just want to get behind them and push!"

A member of the dive team eyes a sea sponge big enough to sleep inside.

One scientist who really knows what it takes to survive in Antarctica is Gerald Kooyman from the Scripps Institution of Oceanography. He spends ten weeks every other year camping on the ice near McMurdo Station to study the deep-diving ability of seals and emperor penguins. It's a big change from the beaches near his home in Southern California.

Gerald and his research group have made many interesting discoveries. Unlike other penguins, emperor penguins are the only penguins to winter over on the antarctic ice. They were thought to stay close to their home colonies all year long. But by attaching electronic backpacks to the penguins' feathers, the researchers found that the birds swim all around the Ross Sea, an area the size of France. They can stay underwater at least 22 minutes and can dive deeper than 1,500 feet (460 meters).

Penguins are designed for life in the sea and on the ice—which is fortunate since these birds can't fly. A streamlined body, paddle-like feet, and a layer of blubber beneath watertight feathers make penguins speedy and comfortable underwater. As penguins preen their feathers, they spread oil from a gland near their tail that waterproofs them.

Feathers also help to regulate their body temperature on land. When penguins feel cold they turn their black backs toward the sun to absorb its warmth. They face the sun with their white chests when they want to cool down. Bill remembers photographing a group of Adélie penguins sunning themselves on a chunk of sea ice, their white bibs turned toward the sun. Suddenly a leopard seal leaped onto the ice behind them and, startled, the flock turned as one to face the predator. The seal managed to grab a penguin near the edge of the ice. It dove back into the water with its prey. This triggered a panic among the remaining penguins but none of them dared to jump off the ice into the water.

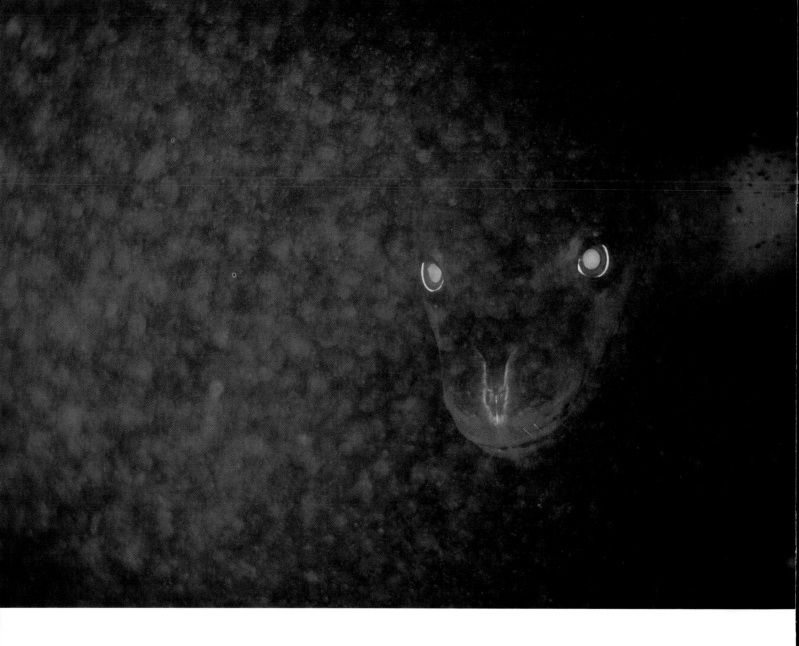

The leopard seal emerged from the shadows at 120 feet below the surface.

Bill himself recalls a close encounter with a leopard seal. It happened on a day when Bill's camera wasn't working right. The flash attachment, called a strobe light, was misfiring, flashing on and off continuously. Bill was diving 120 feet below the surface and there wasn't anything he could do to fix it, so he kept the strobe behind him where it wouldn't blind the scientist trying to do his work. Suddenly Bill felt a tug on his strobe light. He turned around to come face to face with a big leopard seal! Bill yanked the strobe away from the curious animal and thinking quickly, flashed a photo!

Then a flock of emperor penguins zoomed by. Each bird left a trail of bubbles as the water pressure squeezed out the air trapped between their feathers. The leopard seal took off in pursuit. This predator spends the winter feeding on krill, but in the spring, when the penguins are hunting for food for their chicks, the leopard seal feasts on the fatty birds.

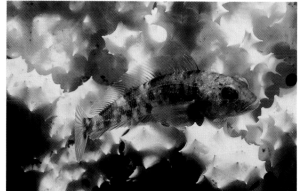

The ice fish has antifreeze in its veins.

Although there are more than 20,000 species of fish in the world, only 120 kinds can live in cold antarctic waters. Bill knows that most fish are cold-blooded and take on the temperature of the surrounding water. So how do these fish keep from freezing in sub-freezing water? He learns that one fish in particular is well suited for life in antarctic waters.

The antarctic ice fish has a natural antifreeze that runs through its veins instead of red blood. (Red blood cells don't carry oxygen well in low temperatures.) It also has a large heart and wide blood vessels to help pump its thin, clear blood through its body. Its colorless blood gives the ice fish a pale, ghostly appearance. Bill has heard that antarctic whalers used to call it the white crocodile fish because of its large mouth with many long teeth.

Antarctica's ice is important to creatures living below it and on top of it. Like a lid covering the ocean, it keeps heat in so the water is always warmer than the air. The underside of the ice supports a marine meadow of microscopic plants that feed krill and the rest of the antarctic food web. The top side provides a relatively safe refuge for penguins from leopard seals—a place where the birds can rest, nest, and raise their young. When there are changes in the sea ice—either from natural cycles or brought on by human activities—the effects are felt in Antarctica and far away.

We now know that the penguin population and the krill population rise and fall depending on the amount of ice surrounding Antarctica in the winter. For nearly thirty years, Susan and Wayne Trivelpiece have been studying Adélie penguins on King George Island near the tip of the Antarctic Peninsula. Susan explains, "If the sea ice is heavy and extends over large areas where the krill spawn, then most of the newly hatched krill will survive and there will be enough food for the young penguins."

But winter temperatures on the peninsula have risen about 4° to 5°F (15°C) over the last fifty years, changing the sea ice distribution. The Trivelpieces have recorded a 50 percent decline in Adélie penguins returning to their study site, and they think that the young penguins are not getting enough food because there are fewer krill.

Other penguin colonies are threatened by too much ice. On the opposite side of Antarctica, several huge icebergs have broken away from the Ross Ice Shelf and piled up in the Ross Sea. Now, instead of swimming from their feeding grounds to their nesting grounds, thousands of adult Adélie penguins have to walk across the ice, a trip that can take five times as long. Scientists believe that many won't survive the long march.

Changes in Antarctica also affect other parts of the world because this continent of ice is like a global air conditioner. Winds and currents flowing away from Antarctica circulate cool temperatures around the earth. Heavy, salty water, called Antarctic Bottom Water can be traced all the way to the North Pole. Slightly warmer, fresher water from the melting of the ice sheet, called Antarctic Intermediate Water, can be found as far north as New York City!

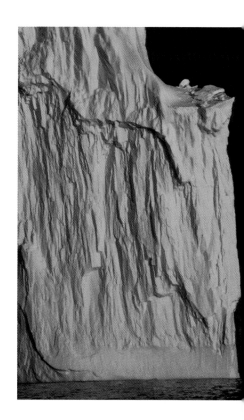

Even in faraway Antarctica, scientists may be seeing evidence of global warming. Temperature differences of just a few degrees can start changes. Ice sheets are breaking apart. The Ross Sea, the saltiest sea in the Southern Ocean, is becoming less salty because of reduced sea ice and melting of the West Antarctic Ice Sheet.

There are other changes, too. In 1985 scientists discovered that there was a hole in the thin ozone layer of the atmosphere 7 to 15 miles above Antarctica. The ozone layer protects the earth from harmful ultraviolet (UV) radiation from the sun. After three years of monitoring, they found the culprit: a group of chemicals called CFCs found in refrigerators, solvents, and spray cans could destroy ozone even as far away as above Antarctica. Higher UV radiation has been linked to increases in skin cancer in humans and may cause changes to the phytoplankton and krill, which affects all the animals within the antarctic food web.

But in spite of these changes, Antarctica has the distinction of still being the most peaceful, untouched place on earth. No wars have ever been fought there, no country owns it, and tourists and scientists don't need to have a passport or anyone's permission to visit. This Zone of Peace offers researchers from different fields and different countries something very rare: the chance to cooperate and learn more about this continent and the world beyond. Because it is cleaner than anywhere else on earth, Antarctica is an ideal outdoor laboratory for studying weather, the stars, climate change, and human impacts on the environment. Its desolate surface even serves as a training area for Mars exploration.

Seals huddle together on the antarctic ice.

As the last natural wilderness, Antarctica still lures those seeking adventure. Too much so, worries Bill Curtsinger, who has seen the impact of more tourists and even scientists on the continent. "About 15,000 tourists and 4,000 scientists visit Antarctica each year. By 2010 it's projected that 1.5 million people a season will come to Antarctica. How can we make sure they don't destroy the very qualities they are coming to experience?"

A new kind of research is now taking place in Antarctica, called the Human Impacts Research Program. These scientists, mostly from Australia, study the impact of visitors and vehicles such as helicopters, snowmobiles, and Zodiacs invading the breeding sites of seals, petrels, and penguins. They are also examining ways to clean up abandoned worksites without causing more damage. Until the mid-1980s the preferred way of disposing of garbage was to push it out onto the sea ice. When the ice broke up in spring, the debris would go away. All of us now know that there is no "away."

Their work is leading to new rules of conduct for tourists and scientists to make sure that wildlife and this unique frozen wilderness are disturbed as little as possible.

Even those of us who will never visit Antarctica can appreciate the value in keeping it as natural and unspoiled as possible. The countries of the world have agreed that Antarctica will remain free—from oil drilling, exploitation, and war. It's important to preserve wild places where our imaginations can roam free.

LET'S FIND OUT MORE

There are many ways to find out about Antarctica without actually going there—through books and the Internet.

WEBSITES

- **Antarctica: The Farthest Place Close to Home:** www.amnh.org/education/resources/antarctica/index.php This rich curriculum resource has been put together by the American Museum of Natural History. Each curriculum material includes a timeline, teacher strategies for implementing activities and readings in the classroom, suggestions for final projects in which students apply their new skills and knowledge, and National Science and Social Studies Standards correlation. Topics include: Continent of Extremes; Day and Night Cycles; Extreme Temperatures; Extreme Winds; Maps; Exploration; Navigation and GPS; Organisms; and Hazards to Humans.

- **Classroom Antarctica:** http://classroomantarctica.aad.gov.au/

- **Gulf of Maine Aquarium:** www.gma.org

- **Space Available, Antarctica Live from Antarctica2:** http://quest.arc.nasa.gov/antarctica2/index.html

- **Antarctic Facts:** www.coolantarctica.com

- **Teachers Experiencing Antarctica and the Artic:** http://tea.rice.edu TEA is a program sponsored by the National Science Foundation (NSF) in which teachers are selected to travel to the Antarctic and the Arctic for a field season to participate in ongoing research. TEA is a partnership between teachers, researchers, students, school districts, and communities. The website includes online journals from teachers in the field, classroom activities and links to websites on education, polar research, and exploration.

READ ABOUT IT

Cerullo, Mary. **Ocean Detectives: Solving the Mysteries of the Sea**. Austin, TX: Raintree Steck-Vaughn, 2000.

Chester, Jonathan. **A for Antarctica**. Berkeley, CA: Tricycle Press, 1998.

Dewey, Jennifer Owings. **Antarctic Journal: Four Months at the Bottom of the World**. New York: HarperCollins, 2001.

McMillan, Bruce. **Summer Ice: Life Along the Antarctic Peninsula**. Boston: Houghton Mifflin, 1995.

Potter, Keith R. **Seven Weeks on an Iceberg**. San Francisco: Chronicle Books, 1999.

GLOSSARY

anchor ice This ice forms as colder, fresh water sinks to the ocean floor and freezes on whatever it touches, including rocks, mud, or bottom animals. pp 10, 11

auger A tool with a spiral cutting edge to bore holes in wood, ice, earth, etc. p 3

bends (decompression sickness) A condition that may occur in a diver when gas in the bloodstream from breathing compressed air is released too quickly, like removing the cap from a bottle of carbonated water. p 8

benthic Bottom-dwelling. pp 2, 10

CFCs (chlorofluorocarbons) A group of chemicals found in refrigerators, solvents, and spray cans which can destroy ozone. p 33

continental ice sheet An ice sheet formed from snow accumulating, year after year, until it compresses into ice. This forms glaciers, which can move slowly down mountain valleys. Antarctic ice sheets are 12,000 feet (3,658 meters) thick in places. pp 1, 33

ecologist A scientist who studies the relationships among plants, animals, and their environment. p 13

fast ice Ice that is attached to the land. It never melts. There is water beneath it.

food web A complex interrelationship of who eats whom. pp 19, 33

gigantism A condition found around the poles in which normally small marine creatures grow to unusually large size. pp 20, 21

global warming The theory that carbon dioxide and other gases produced by the burning of fossil fuels are trapped in the upper atmosphere, absorbing and reflecting heat back to earth. p 33

iceberg A mass of ice broken off from a glacier and floating in the sea. p 31

isopod A small crustacean that resembles a shrimp with a flat, oval body. p 20

krill Small, shrimp-like creatures that exist in huge numbers in antarctic waters (and elsewhere). They are important food for many other animals. pp 18-19, 27, 33

ozone hole A hole in a thin ozone layer that protects the earth from harmful ultraviolet (UV) radiation from the sun. p 33

pack ice Broken pieces of sea ice that have pushed together into one big mass of ice. This is where seals give birth to their pups.

peninsula Land surrounded on three sides by water.

phytoplankton Microscopic plants that drift with the ocean currents. pp 7, 19, 33

predator An animal that eats other animals. p 23

rime ice A coating of tiny ice crystals that forms on grass, leaves, etc. from moisture in the air. p 15

sea ice Formed by the freezing of sea water. Sea ice floats on the surface of the water. Under the stress of wind and ocean currents, sea ice cracks and moves. Sea ice is also called annual ice, because it breaks up in summer. As the temperature warms, it becomes too dangerous to try to drive vehicles on it. pp 1, 10, 23, 28, 31, 33, 35

shelf ice Continental ice that flows out from the land to the sea surface and floats on the ocean. It can be 1,640 feet (500 meters) thick in places. pp 1, 33

solvent A liquid that dissolves another substance; a powerful cleaning solution. p 33

ultraviolet radiation (UV) Light rays that produce harmful effects on humans, animals, and phytoplankton. p 33

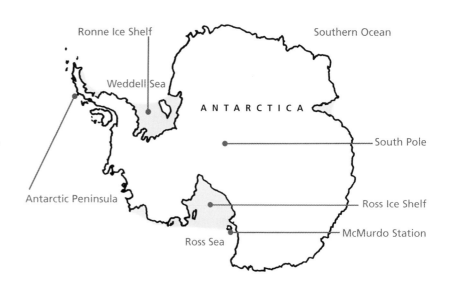

TILBURY HOUSE, PUBLISHERS

2 Mechanic Street, Gardiner, Maine 04345

800–582–1899 • www.tilburyhouse.com

Our thanks to: Karen Baker, Ph.D., Long-Term Ecological Research Program/Information Management, for reviewing the manuscript; Baldo Marinovic, Institute of Marine Sciences, University of California, Santa Cruz; Paul Dayton, Ph.D., Scripps Institute of Oceanography; Charles Galt, Biological Sciences, University of California Long Beach; Myles Gordon, Ed.D., Director of Education, American Museum of Natural History, for curriculum guidance; Terry Klinger, Ph.D., University of Washington School of Marine Affairs; National Geographic Image Sales for the use of Bill Curtsinger's photo of the leopard seal at the top of page 26; the staff and advisory board of the National Science Foundation and its Teachers Experiencing the Arctic and Antarctica Program (TEA) for inspiration; and Gordon Robilliard, Entrix Biological Consultants.

Library of Congress Cataloging-in-Publication Data

Cerullo, Mary M.

Life under ice / Mary M. Cerullo ; photography by Bill Curtsinger.

p. cm.

Summary: Follows marine photographer Bill Curtsinger as he dives under the ice at Antarctica to learn about the plants and animals that thrive in this extreme habitat.

ISBN 0-88448-246-4 (hardcover : alk. paper)

1. Marine organisms—Antarctica—Juvenile literature.   [1. Marine animals—Antarctica.

2. Marine plants—Antarctica. 3. Antarctica.]   I. Curtsinger, Bill, 1946-   , ill. II. Title.

QH84.2.C47 2003

578.777—dc21

2002154451

Designed by Geraldine Millham, Westport, MA

Editorial and production work by Jennifer Bunting, Audrey Maynard, and Barbara Diamond.

Color scans by Integrated Composition Systems, Spokane, WA

Printing and binding by Worzalla Publishing, Stevens Point, WI